Table of Contents

Spelling Week 1 – Words with a Short *a* Sound 2

Spelling Week 2 – Words with a Short *e* Sound 5

Spelling Week 3 – Words with a Short *i* Sound..................................... 8

Spelling Week 4 – Words with a Short *o* Sound 11

Spelling Week 5 – Words with a Short *u* Sound 14

Spelling Week 6 – Words with a Long *a* Sound 17

Spelling Week 7 – Words with a Long *e* Sound................................... 20

Spelling Week 8 – Words with a Long *i* Sound 23

Spelling Week 9 – Words with a Long *o* Sound................................... 26

Spelling Week 10 – Words with a Long *u* Sound................................. 29

Spelling Week 11 – Words with *y* as Long *i* and Long *e* Sounds 32

Spelling Week 12 – Contractions.. 35

Spelling Week 13 – Double Consonants... 38

Spelling Week 14 – Words That End in Double Consonants............... 41

Spelling Week 15 – Words That End in Silent *e* 44

Spelling Week 16 – Words with Long and Short *oo* Sounds............... 47

Spelling Week 17 – Compound Words 50

Spelling Week 18 – Words with *oi* and *oy* 53

Spelling Week 19 – Words with an *s* Sound 56

Spelling Week 20 – Words with a *j* Sound 59

Spelling Week 21 – Words with *ow* and *ou* 62

Spelling Week 22 – Months of the Year.. 65

Spelling Week 23 – Consonant Digraphs *ch*, *sh*, *th*, and *wh*................68

Spelling Week 24 – Consonant Blends *scr*, *spl*, *spr*, and *str*...............71

Spelling Week 25 – Easily Misspelled Words..74

Spelling Week 26 – R-controlled Vowels with *or*, *er*, *ir*, *ur*, and *ear*........77

Spelling Week 27 – R-controlled Vowels with *ar*, *are*, *or*, and *ore*.........80

Spelling Week 28 – Words with an f Sound Spelled *ph*, *gh*, and *f* 83

Spelling Week 29 – Words with Silent Letters.......................................86

Spelling Week 30 – Homophones 89

Spelling Tests 92

Everyday Words to Know How to Spell 107

Spelling Practice Menu...110

Word Search Template 111

Spelling Tracker..112

Answers..113

Certificates 120

Steps for Learning Spelling Words

1. Look carefully at the spelling word.
2. Say the spelling word out loud.
   - How many syllables do you hear?
   - What consonant sounds do you hear?
   - What vowel sounds do you hear?
3. Check the spelling word for spelling patterns.
4. Spell the spelling word out loud.
5. Cover the spelling word.
6. Write the spelling word from memory.
7. Check the spelling word.
8. Repeat as needed.

Spelling Week 1 – Words with a Short *a* Sound

Say each word out loud. Listen for the short *a* sound.

Copy and spell each word three times using colors of your choice.

1. about _____ _____ _____

2. ask _____ _____ _____

3. stand _____ _____ _____

4. catch _____ _____ _____

5. away _____ _____ _____

6. than _____ _____ _____

7. brand _____ _____ _____

8. class _____ _____ _____

9. after _____ _____ _____

10. apple _____ _____ _____

Brain Stretch

- Create a word search puzzle based on the spelling words.
- On a piece of paper, write a sentence using each spelling word.

Spelling Week 1 – Words with a Short *a* Sound

about	after	apple	ask	away
brand	catch	class	stand	than

1. Fill in the blank using the best spelling word from the list.

   a) Kim shared an _____ with her friend Dawn.

   b) My dog has a favorite _____ of dog food.

   c) Josh brought his net to _____ bugs in the field.

   d) Grandma is going _____ for the winter.

   e) Tina's book is _____ furry pets.

   f) The _____ planted a garden in the schoolyard.

   g) My cat is bigger _____ your dog!

   h) I will do my homework _____ I eat a snack.

   i) Sasha has to _____ on tiptoe to reach the shelf.

   j) Jack is going to _____ a question.

Brain Stretch

How many spelling words can you fit into one sentence and still make sense? Give it a try!

Spelling Week 1 – Word Study

To make many **nouns** plural, just add the letter **s**.

Examples: trap – traps   band – bands   crab – crabs

For some nouns, you need to do something different.

Watch for nouns like the ones below.

Nouns ending with…	**To make the noun plural…**
s, x, ch, or **sh**	Add **es**
	Example: one dash – two dashes

1. Change the singular nouns to a plural noun.

   a) house _____   b) lash _____   c) pass _____

   d) batch _____   e) flash _____   f) glass _____

   g) box _____   h) truck _____   i) peach _____

2. How many syllables does the word have? Write the number beside the word.

   a) kangaroo _____   b) fast _____   c) caterpillar _____

3. What does **park** mean in the sentence? Circle the correct definition.

   Dad had to park across the street.

   a green place   leave a vehicle in a spot

Spelling Week 2 – Words with a Short *e* Sound

Say each word out loud. Listen for the short *e* sound.

Copy and spell each word three times using colors of your choice.

1. forget _____ _____ _____

2. help _____ _____ _____

3. else _____ _____ _____

4. dress _____ _____ _____

5. test _____ _____ _____

6. next _____ _____ _____

7. best _____ _____ _____

8. vent _____ _____ _____

9. said _____ _____ _____

10. friend _____ _____ _____

Spelling Tip

The short *e* sound can be spelled with *ai* (*said*) or *ie* (*friend*).

Spelling Week 2 – Words with a Short *e* Sound

| best | dress | else | forget | friend |
| help | next | said | test | vent |

1. Fill in the blank using the best spelling word from the list.

   a) Cam entered his _____ story in the writing contest.

   b) Mary _____ her cat had a litter of kittens yesterday.

   c) My family is going to _____ my aunt and uncle move.

   d) _____ weekend, it will be my birthday.

   e) James is Tony's best _____.

   f) Jenny dropped her quarter down the heating _____.

   g) Make sure you study for the spelling _____ tomorrow.

   h) I must not _____ my umbrella today.

   i) Timmy wanted to add something _____ to his drawing.

   j) Ana wore a new _____ to the birthday party.

Brain Stretch

How many spelling words can you fit into one sentence and still make sense? Give it a try!

Spelling Week 2 – Word Study

1. Underline the word with the short **e** sound. Write the word on the line.

   a)   chick   letter   rich   nose   life   _____

   b)   school   click   spread   love   pass   _____

   c)   money   store   fuzz   lift   sled   _____

   d)   trash   lend   carry   first   half   _____

   e)   screen   ear   line   said   scarf   _____

2. Circle the word with the short **e** sound that makes the most sense.
   Write the word in the sentence.

   a) Mark _____ to the store to buy bread for lunch. (lend went)

   b) Yu entered her _____ drawing in the art contest. (pet's best)

   c) When she is hungry, my uncle's dog barks until she is _____. (fed red)

   d) That rooster has a tall, red _____ on its head. (crest vest)

3. The word **shed** can have two meanings.
   Write a sentence to show each meaning of the word **shed**.

   _____

   _____

Spelling Week 3 – Words with a Short *i* Sound

Say each word out loud. Listen for the short *i* sound.

Copy and spell each word three times using colors of your choice.

1. little
2. children
3. pick
4. think
5. drink
6. its
7. slip
8. itch
9. if
10. this

Brain Stretch

- Create a word search puzzle based on the spelling words.
- On a piece of paper, write a sentence using each spelling word.

Spelling Week 3 – Words with a Short *i* Sound

| children | drink | if | itch | its |
| little | pick | slip | think | this |

1. Fill in the blank using the best spelling word from the list.

   a) A group of _____ sat and listened to the story.

   b) The _____ girl lost her mitten on the school bus.

   c) My family is going to _____ apples at the orchard.

   d) Be careful you don't _____ on the ice!

   e) _____ is the hottest day of the summer so far!

   f) Jess sat down to _____ of some project ideas.

   g) The dog kept licking _____ paw.

   h) A red bird had a _____ at our new birdbath.

   i) Ask your parents _____ you can sleep over tonight.

   j) A bug bit my arm and it started to _____ badly.

Brain Stretch

How many spelling words can you fit into one sentence and still make sense? Give it a try!

Spelling Week 3 – Word Study

To make some nouns plural, you need to do something different. Watch for nouns like the ones below.

Nouns ending with…

consonant + y

To make the noun plural…

Change **y** to **i** and add **es**

Example: one kitty — two kitties

1. Change the singular nouns to a plural noun.

   a) family _____   b) fifty _____   c) city _____

   d) giveaway _____ e) piggy _____   f) display _____

   g) hippy _____   h) story _____   i) memory _____

2. How many syllables does the word have? Write the number beside the word.

   a) spaceship _____ b) hippopotamus _____ c) twins _____

3. The word **bat** can have two meanings.

   Write a sentence to show each meaning of the word **bat**.

   _____

   _____

Spelling Week 4 – Words with a Short *o* Sound

Say each word out loud. Listen for the short *o* sound.

Copy and spell each word three times using colors of your choice.

1. rot
2. hot
3. shop
4. body
5. spot
6. pond
7. odd
8. lots
9. rock
10. drop

Brain Stretch

- Create a word search puzzle based on the spelling words.
- On a piece of paper, write a sentence using each spelling word.

Spelling Week 4 – Words with a Short *o* Sound

body	drop	hot	lots	odd
pond	rock	rot	shop	spot

1. Fill in the blank using the best spelling word from the list.

   a) Tess said the split tomato was starting to _____.

   b) Mike found a beautiful shiny _____ at the beach.

   c) Frogs, snails, and minnows all live in the _____.

   d) The strawberry left a red _____ on my shirt.

   e) My mother and I _____ for food on Fridays.

   f) Dad cooked pancakes on the _____ griddle.

   g) The doll I knitted has a very lumpy _____ shape.

   h) If I ask Bruno to give me the ball, he will _____ it.

   i) Patty is wearing a very _____ triangle hat today.

   j) We gave _____ of clothing to the charity store.

Brain Stretch

How many spelling words can you fit into one sentence and still make sense? Give it a try!

Spelling Week 4 – Word Study

For nouns that end in **s, x, ch,** or **sh,** you need to add **es** to make them plural.

Nouns ending with…
s, x, ch, or sh

To make the noun plural…
Add **es**
Example: one wish – two wishes

1. Change the singular nouns to a plural noun.

   a) box _____ b) porch _____ c) moss _____

   d) torch _____ e) boss _____ f) slosh _____

   g) gloss _____ h) sandbox _____ i) sash _____

2. Write two words that rhyme with the word **rot**.
   The words don't have to be spelled the same.

   _____

3. The word **fair** can have two meanings.
   Write a sentence to show each meaning of the word **fair**.

   _____

   _____

Spelling Week 5 – Words with a Short *u* Sound

Say each word out loud. Look at the different letters that make the short *u* sound. Copy and spell each word three times using colors of your choice.

1. munch   _____   _____   _____

2. such   _____   _____   _____

3. cut   _____   _____   _____

4. under   _____   _____   _____

5. buzz   _____   _____   _____

6. summer   _____   _____   _____

7. lunch   _____   _____   _____

8. month   _____   _____   _____

9. Monday   _____   _____   _____

10. mother   _____   _____   _____

Spelling Tip

Words with *o* can have a short *u* sound (*Monday, month, mother*).

Spelling Week 5 – Words with a Short *u* Sound

buzz	cut	lunch	Monday	month
mother	munch	stuffing	summer	under

1. Fill in the blank using the best spelling word from the list.

   a) The bees _____ all around the spring flowers.

   b) Bruno ripped all the _____ out of his teddy bear.

   c) My friend's _____ makes good cheese sandwiches.

   d) Tim dropped a quarter and it rolled _____ the bed.

   e) Kate helped her father _____ vegetables for dinner.

   f) I love to watch my rabbit _____ on lettuce.

   g) This _____, I will take swimming lessons.

   h) In what _____ is your birthday?

   i) We are going to the dentist on _____.

   j) My sister and I had leftover pizza for _____ today.

Brain Stretch

How many spelling words can you fit into one sentence and still make sense? Give it a try!

Spelling Week 5 – Word Study

1. Circle the words that do **not** have a short *u* sound.

   a) punch   couch   touch   tough   through

   b) ground   flutter   bounce   drum   must

   c) fluff   pout   beauty   putter   sponge

   d) grouch   bump   tumble   rough   guest

   e) love   above   cove   smudge   about

2. Use a letter or letters from the list below to make words that have the short *u* sound. Say the word out loud. Write the letter or letters on the line.

   c   **d**   **gl**   **f**   **r**   **fl**   **b**   **st**   **t**

   a) _____utter   b) _____over   c) _____ove

   d) _____ough   e) _____udge   f) _____uff

   g) _____ump   h) _____ouch   i) _____ouble

Spelling Week 6 – Words with a Long *a* Sound

Say each word out loud. Listen for the long *a* sound.

Copy and spell each word three times using colors of your choice.

1. play _____ _____ _____

2. came _____ _____ _____

3. lake _____ _____ _____

4. save _____ _____ _____

5. sway _____ _____ _____

6. tale _____ _____ _____

7. paint _____ _____ _____

8. mail _____ _____ _____

9. today _____ _____ _____

10. snail _____ _____ _____

Spelling Tips: The long *a* sound can be spelled with
- letters *ai* (*mail*)
- letter *a* with a consonant and *e* (*make*)
- letters *ay* (*hay*)

Spelling Week 6 – Words with a Long *a* Sound

| came | lake | mail | paint | play |
| save | snail | sway | tale | today |

1. Fill in the blank using the best spelling word from the list.

   a) The wind grew strong, and the trees began to _____.

   b) My mother is going to _____ my bedroom light green.

   c) Sam and her friends _____ tag in the park after school.

   d) His grandparents took him fishing in the _____ at the cottage.

   e) The old man told a _____ of adventure in the forest.

   f) Fran's cousins _____ to her birthday party.

   g) A huge _____ ate my mother's bean plants.

   h) My little brother loves to see what comes in the _____.

   i) If I _____ my money, I can buy the book I want.

   j) The sun is shining, and it is very warm outside _____.

Brain Stretch

How many spelling words can you fit into one sentence and still make sense? Give it a try!

Spelling Week 6 – Word Study

1. Say the word out loud. Underline the words with the long *a* sound.

   a) break   late   meat   bait   peach

   b) face   batch   lazy   peace   state

   c) paste   neat   grate   case   coat

   d) read   play   made   capital   sway

   e) greet   clay   start   gate   eight

2. Write the letters of the alphabet that have a long *a* sound in their name.

   _____

3. Write the numbers between 1 and 100 that have a long *a* sound in their name.

   _____

   _____

   _____

Spelling Week 7 – Words with a Long *e* Sound

Say each word out loud. Look at the different letters that make the long **e** sound. Copy and spell each word three times using colors of your choice.

1. sweet _____ _____ _____

2. street _____ _____ _____

3. treat _____ _____ _____

4. speed _____ _____ _____

5. please _____ _____ _____

6. each _____ _____ _____

7. these _____ _____ _____

8. team _____ _____ _____

9. easy _____ _____ _____

10. theme _____ _____ _____

Spelling Tips: The long e sound can be spelled with
- letter **e** by itself, and **e** followed by a **consonant + e** (*evil, even*)
- letters **ee**, **ea**, and **ie** (*eel, speak, field*)
- letter **y** (*puppy*)

Spelling Week 7 – Words with a Long *e* Sound

each	easy	please	speed	street
sweet	team	theme	these	treat

1. Fill in the blank using the best spelling word from the list.

   a) Jim says his homework was _____ today.

   b) My cousins play ball hockey on the _____.

   c) Watermelon is bright pink and very _____.

   d) Our dog Max gets a _____ when he does a trick.

   e) _____ dishes need to be put away.

   f) Tasha joined the soccer _____ yesterday

   g) My brother's running _____ is very fast.

   h) Always remember to say _____ and thank you.

   i) There are five eggs in _____ nest.

   j) The party had a pirate _____.

Brain Stretch

How many spelling words can you fit into one sentence and still make sense? Give it a try!

Spelling Week 7 – Word Study

> To make these nouns plural, remember this rule:
>
> If the noun ends with a **consonant + y**, change **y** to **i** and add **es**.

1. Change the singular nouns to a plural noun.

   a) story _____   b) puppy _____   c) carry _____

   d) hurry _____   e) baby _____   f) berry _____

   g) family _____   h) party _____   i) daisy _____

2. How many syllables does the word have? Write the number beside the word.

   a) extreme _____   b) sweet _____   c) Japanese _____

3. Which province has a long **e** sound in its name? Write the name.

   _____

4. Make three compound words using these words with a long **e** sound.

   ever   jelly   sitter   baby   green   bean

   _____

   _____

Spelling Week 8 – Words with a Long *i* Sound

Say each word out loud. Listen for the long *i* sound.

Copy and spell each word three times using colors of your choice.

1. fine _____ _____ _____

2. night _____ _____ _____

3. spice _____ _____ _____

4. twice _____ _____ _____

5. like _____ _____ _____

6. pile _____ _____ _____

7. high _____ _____ _____

8. dry _____ _____ _____

9. spy _____ _____ _____

10. tie _____ _____ _____

Spelling Tips: The long *i* sound can be spelled with

- letters *igh* and *ign* (*bright*, *design*)
- letter *i* followed by **consonant + e** (*dive*)
- letters *ie* and *y* (*pie*, *buy*)

Spelling Week 8 – Words with a Long *i* Sound

| dry | fine | high | like | night |
| pile | spice | spy | tie | twice |

1. Fill in the blank using the best spelling word from the list.

   a) I called my dog _____ but he didn't come in.

   b) Bob loves to look up at the stars at _____.

   c) My favorite _____ is cinnamon.

   d) Sandy always plays a _____ when we play dress-up.

   e) My father can climb very _____ on the ladder.

   f) We fold the laundry when it is _____.

   g) Vicky's baby brother learned to _____ his shoes.

   h) Grandpa was sick last week, but now he's _____.

   i) I _____ to draw pictures of animals.

   j) We jumped in a huge _____ of leaves in our yard.

Brain Stretch

How many spelling words can you fit into one sentence and still make sense? Give it a try!

Spelling Week 8 – Word Study

1. Say the word out loud. Underline the words with the long *i* sound.

   a) spine   pink   sign   guy   fly

   b) tint   kind   iron   skill   hind

   c) special   slip   rise   eye   twin

   d) twine   mine   twice   lit   white

   e) grind   grin   sink   mail   wipe

2. A **synonym** is a word that means the same as another word.

   Circle the synonym for the bolded word.

   a) **fine**   okay   upset   b) **sly**   scared   sneaky

3. An **antonym** is a word that has the opposite meaning of another word.

   Circle the antonym for the bolded word.

   a) **mine**   yours   his   b) **find**   discover   lose

4. Write the number words from one to ten that have a long *i* sound.

   _____

5. For each number word from Question 4, write a word that rhymes with it.

   _____

Spelling Week 9 – Words with a Long *o* Sound

Say each word out loud. Look at the different letters that make the long *o* sound. Copy and spell each word three times using colors of your choice.

1. coat _____ _____ _____

2. gold _____ _____ _____

3. slow _____ _____ _____

4. coach _____ _____ _____

5. bone _____ _____ _____

6. almost _____ _____ _____

7. loaf _____ _____ _____

8. grow _____ _____ _____

9. alone _____ _____ _____

10. both _____ _____ _____

Spelling Tips: A long *o* sound can be made with
- letter *o* (*troll, bonus, go*)
- letters *oe* (*toe*)
- letters *oa* and *ow* (*moat, crow*)
- letter *o* followed by a **consonant + e** (*mole*)

Spelling Week 9 – Words with a Long *o* Sound

almost	alone	bone	both	coach
coat	gold	grow	load	show

1. Fill in the blank using the best spelling word from the list.

   a) It took Pam a long time to find _____ her socks.

   b) I _____ ran all the way home, but I got tired.

   c) Every summer, children seem to _____ faster.

   d) The man found a _____ nugget in the river.

   e) Our dog likes to chew on a big beef _____ .

   f) The sad child sat _____ on the swing.

   g) It was cold outside, so Tim wore his _____ .

   h) My friends and I watched a funny _____ on TV.

   i) We helped mom fold a big _____ of dry laundry.

   j) My baseball _____ helps me learn new skills.

Brain Stretch

How many spelling words can you fit into one sentence and still make sense? Give it a try!

Spelling Week 9 – Word Study

1. Underline the words in the story that have a long **o** sound.

   Mario and his family took a trip to the zoo. Most of them were excited to see all the animals. But his cousin Lori didn't want to go. She was afraid of the hippos and polar bears. Her cousin Tony held her hand and told her about each animal as they went. There was so much to learn! When she saw the hippos rolling in the water, she started to laugh. The hippos were having fun! The polar bears were playing with a ball. They were having fun, too! One old bear was sleeping. Lori and her family were safe behind walls the whole time. When they left the zoo, Lori said she couldn't wait to go to the zoo again!

2. A **synonym** is a word that means the same as another word.

   Circle the synonym for the bolded word.

   a) **goal**   slap   score

   b) **flow**   run   plant

3. An **antonym** is a word that has the opposite meaning of another word.

   Circle the antonym for the bolded word.

   a) **narrow**   wide   skinny

   b) **float**   grow   sink

4. How many syllables does the word have? Write the number on the line.

   a) tomorrow _____   b) elbow _____   c) troll _____

5. What does **throw** mean in the sentence? Circle the correct definition.

   My grandmother knitted a throw for my bed.

   to toss something   a type of blanket

Spelling Week 10 – Words with a Long *u* Sound

Say each word out loud. Look at the different letters that make the long *u* sound.
Copy and spell each word three times using colors of your choice.

1. use _____   _____   _____

2. chew _____   _____   _____

3. unicorn _____   _____   _____

4. pure _____   _____   _____

5. cube _____   _____   _____

6. cute _____   _____   _____

7. argue _____   _____   _____

8. fuse _____   _____   _____

9. huge _____   _____   _____

10. value _____   _____   _____

Spelling Tips: A long *u* sound can be made with

- letter *u* followed by a **consonant** + **e** (*use*)
- letter *u* followed by a **consonant** + *i* or *y* (*cupid, duty*)
- letters **ue** (*due*)
- letters **ew** (*few, ewe*)

Spelling Week 10 – Words with a Long *u* Sound

| argue | chew | cube | cute | fuse |
| huge | pure | unicorn | use | value |

1. Fill in the blank using the best spelling word from the list.

   a) Aunt Zo asked if I wanted a _____ of sugar in my tea.

   b) The girl wanted a rainbow _____ toy for her present.

   c) Four _____ kittens mewed in their basket.

   d) The men started to _____ over who owned the paper.

   e) The stove overheated and blew a _____.

   f) Grandma says you should always _____ your food well.

   g) _____, clean water flowed from the spring in the ground.

   h) Six muffins for $1.50 was a great _____.

   i) The T-rex skeleton at the museum was _____!

   j) Ted had to _____ all his strength to push open the heavy door.

Brain Stretch

How many spelling words can you fit into one sentence and still make sense? Give it a try!

Spelling Week 10 – Word Study

These words with a long *u* sound have been cut apart by mistake!
You can help put them back together.

1. Say the first part of the word out loud.

    Choose a second part. Say it with the first part to see if it makes sense.

    Draw a line from the first part of the word to the second part.

    Print the words on the lines at the bottom of the page.

    a) ar   ew

    b) ew   ue

    c) cu   e

    d) tr   gue

    e) f   cue

    f) res   be

a) _____ b) _____ c) _____

d) _____ e) _____ f) _____

Spelling Week 11 – Words with *y* as Long *i* and Long *e* Sounds

Say each word out loud. Listen for the long *i* and long *e* sounds.

Copy and spell each word three times using colors of your choice.

1. jelly _____ _____ _____

2. story _____ _____ _____

3. shy _____ _____ _____

4. very _____ _____ _____

5. cry _____ _____ _____

6. sunny _____ _____ _____

7. fly _____ _____ _____

8. family _____ _____ _____

9. why _____ _____ _____

10. dry _____ _____ _____

Brain Stretch

- Create a word search puzzle based on the spelling words.
- On a piece of paper, write a sentence using each spelling word.

Spelling Week 11 – Words with *y* as Long *i* and Long *e* Sounds

| cry | dry | family | fly | jelly |
| shy | story | sunny | very | why |

1. Fill in the blank using the best spelling word from the list.

   a) My cat loves to lay in the warm sunshine on a _____ day.

   b) Our teacher showed us _____ we should reduce, reuse, and recycle.

   c) Cindy's baby boy did not _____ when he was born.

   d) Greg's favorite sandwich is peanut butter and _____.

   e) Most of the time, I am a _____ happy person.

   f) There is a _____ in the fruit salad!

   g) I use a big, fluffy towel to _____ off after my bath.

   h) My whole _____ loves to hike in the forest.

   i) The Elder told us the _____ of Turtle Island.

   j) The little girl next door is very _____.

Brain Stretch

How many spelling words can you fit into one sentence and still make sense? Give it a try!

Spelling Week 11 – Word Study

1. Read the sentence clue. Unscramble the word and write it in the space.

   a) Our dog has fleas, so she is very _____. (ythci)

   b) Joe comes from a big _____ with lots of cousins. (myalif)

   c) Katy is learning to _____ eggs for breakfast. (rfy)

   d) On a clear night, I like to look up at the stars in the _____. (kys)

   e) The dog chased the hen, and now she is very _____. (gynar)

   f) The spoon we used in the honey jar is very _____. (cytisk)

2. Circle the compound words. Write the two words that make the word

   a) butterfly   angry   crying   frypan   carry

   _____

   b) dragonfly   berry   monkey   apply   jellybean

   _____

   c) copying   marry   display   eyeball   skyline

   _____

34

Spelling Week 12 – Contractions

Say each word out loud. Think about what letter or letters are missing.

Copy and spell each word three times using colors of your choice.

1. isn't _____ _____ _____

2. he's _____ _____ _____

3. you'll _____ _____ _____

4. we've _____ _____ _____

5. didn't _____ _____ _____

6. there's _____ _____ _____

7. I'd _____ _____ _____

8. we're _____ _____ _____

9. would'nt _____ _____ _____

10. that's _____ _____ _____

Brain Stretch

- Create a word search puzzle based on the spelling words.
- On a piece of paper, write a sentence using each spelling word.

Spelling Week 12 – Contractions

| didn't | he's | I'd | isn't | that's |
| there's | we're | we've | wouldn't | you'll |

1. Fill in the blank using the best spelling word from the list.

   a) I think _____ like the birthday gift I got you.

   b) If _____ going to the park, Chris wants to bring his ball.

   c) _____ been selling lemonade for charity all summer.

   d) My grandmother said _____ become a good artist.

   e) Dad says _____ a wasp nest in the tree.

   f) Jen thought she _____ like raw peas, but she does!

   g) This is my sister, and _____ my brother.

   h) Ben _____ remember to bring his project to school.

   i) That _____ the way I thought the muffins would turn out.

   j) I love my math teacher. _____ very kind and funny.

Brain Stretch

How many spelling words can you fit into one sentence and still make sense? Give it a try!

Spelling Week 12 – Word Study

There are two tricky contractions. You will have to learn these contractions.

will not = won't   **cannot = can't**

1. Circle the incorrect contraction.
   Write the correct contraction at the end of the sentence.

   a) Emma willn't be coming to my party this weekend. _____

   b) W'ere having pizza for dinner tonight. _____

   c) Iam going to do my homework before I play. _____

   d) Iti's sunny and warm out today. _____

   e) Is that the bus h'es riding in today? _____

2. Read the contraction. Write the words in full.

   Example: I'm   I am

   a) couldn't _____   b) hasn't _____

   c) we're _____   d) she's _____

   e) that's _____   f) can't _____

   g) isn't _____   h) won't _____

   i) you'll _____   j) didn't _____

Spelling Week 13 – Double Consonants

Say each word out loud. Watch for the double consonants.

Copy and spell each word three times using colors of your choice.

1. miss _____ _____ _____

2. soccer _____ _____ _____

3. full _____ _____ _____

4. happen _____ _____ _____

5. funny _____ _____ _____

6. dinner _____ _____ _____

7. better _____ _____ _____

8. buzzer _____ _____ _____

9. zipper _____ _____ _____

10. stuff _____ _____ _____

Brain Stretch

- Create a word search puzzle based on the spelling words.
- On a piece of paper, write a sentence using each spelling word.

Spelling Week 13 – Double Consonants

better	buzzer	dinner	full	funny
happen	miss	soccer	stuff	zipper

1. Fill in the blank using the best spelling word from the list.

   a) Dan got his _____ stuck and couldn't take his jacket off.

   b) Abby is _____ at math than she is at swimming.

   c) My uncle collects all kinds of old _____.

   d) We are having pizza for _____ tonight.

   e) Tina told a very _____ joke in class today.

   f) I wonder what would _____ if we made a volcano.

   g) The _____ went off when the cupcakes were done.

   h) Gabby joined the _____ team this year.

   i) Buster is quite _____ after eating a whole burger.

   j) When school is over for the year, I _____ my friends.

Brain Stretch

How many spelling words can you fit into one sentence and still make sense? Give it a try!

Spelling Week 13 – Word Study

For many verbs that end with **consonant + vowel + consonant**, double the final consonant before adding **ed** or **ing**.

Examples:

Verb	Add ed	Add ing
hop	hopped	hopping
clap	clapped	carry

1. Add **ed** and **ing** to the verb.

   a) chop   _____   _____

   b) knit   _____   _____

   c) drag   _____   _____

   d) skid   _____   _____

   e) rub   _____   _____

2. Circle the words that are spelled correctly. Remember the verb rule.

   a) buildding   sweepping   tripped   calling

   b) washhed   stopping   cookked   smelling

   c) roofing   slipped   missing   liftted

   d) paintted   walkking   chopped   likking

Spelling Week 14 – Words That End in Double Consonants

Say each word out loud. Watch for the double consonants.

Copy and spell each word three times using colors of your choice.

1. spill _____ _____ _____

2. press _____ _____ _____

3. cliff _____ _____ _____

4. bull _____ _____ _____

5. wall _____ _____ _____

6. fluff _____ _____ _____

7. hiss _____ _____ _____

8. grass _____ _____ _____

9. jazz _____ _____ _____

10. doll _____ _____ _____

Brain Stretch

- Create a word search puzzle based on the spelling words.
- On a piece of paper, write a sentence using each spelling word.

Spelling Week 14 – Words That End in Double Consonants

bull	cliff	doll	fluff	grass
hiss	jazz	press	spill	wall

1. Fill in the blank using the best spelling word from the list.

   a) The big snake curled up and started to _____.

   b) My grandmother used to _____ flowers in a book to dry them.

   c) Our neighbors mow their _____ every weekend in summer.

   d) Buster tore apart a pillow and now there is _____ everywhere.

   e) Mom loves to listen to _____ music.

   f) A huge brown _____ is standing in that farmer's field.

   g) Seabirds nest on the _____ beside the ocean.

   h) When I pour a drink, I'm careful not to _____ any.

   i) My baby sister drew on the _____ with a crayon.

   j) Cathy has a favorite _____ that sits on her bed.

Brain Stretch

How many spelling words can you fit into one sentence and still make sense? Give it a try!

Spelling Week 14 – Word Study

1. Write as many words as you can that rhyme with the word below.

   Rhyming words don't have to use the same letters to sound the same.

   a) smell _____

   b) mass _____

   c) scuff _____

   d) mall _____

   e) pull _____

   f) thrill _____

   g) cross _____

   h) roll _____

2. A **synonym** is a word that means the same as another word.

   Circle the synonym for the bolded word.

   a) **well**   sick   healthy   b) **stuff**   fill   fluff

3. An **antonym** is a word that has the opposite meaning of another word.

   Circle the antonym for the bolded word.

   a) **full**   top   empty   b) **tall**   smart   short

Spelling Week 15 – Words That End in Silent *e*

Say each word out loud. Listen to how the silent **e** changes the vowel sounds.

Copy and spell each word three times using colors of your choice.

1. dive   _____   _____   _____

2. save   _____   _____   _____

3. like   _____   _____   _____

4. store _____   _____   _____

5. cute   _____   _____   _____

6. phone _____   _____   _____

7. line   _____   _____   _____

8. shave _____   _____   _____

9. here   _____   _____   _____

10. file _____   _____   _____

Spelling Tip

For many words that end in a vowel followed by a **consonant + silent e**, the *e* makes the vowel say its name.

Spelling Week 15 – Words That End in Silent *e*

cute	dive	file	here	like
line	phone	save	shave	store

1. Fill in the blank using the best spelling word from the list.

   a) The nurse took out a _____ with my name on it.

   b) When frogs spot us, they _____ under the water.

   c) My grandmother calls us on an old _____ in her kitchen.

   d) Kim went to the _____ to buy a loaf of bread.

   e) Fred has started to _____ his beard off.

   f) There are two _____, puppies at the pet store.

   g) I need to _____ my money so I can buy a bicycle.

   h) My mom and I come _____ to watch ducks on the pond.

   i) The boy drew a _____ in the sand with a long stick.

   j) I don't _____ to make mistakes, but I learn from them.

Brain Stretch

How many spelling words can you fit into one sentence and still make sense? Give it a try!

Spelling Week 15 – Word Study

When verbs end with an **e**, drop the **e** before adding **ed** or **ing**.

Examples:

Verb	Add ed	Add ing
bake	baked	baking
shave	shaved	shaving

1. Add **ed** and **ing** to the verb.

   a) skate _____ _____

   b) smile _____ _____

   c) dance _____ _____

   d) hope   _____ _____

   e) save   _____ _____

   f) joke   _____ _____

   g) wave   _____ _____

2. Write the number words from one to ten that end in silent **e**.

   _____

3. For each number word in Question 2, write a word that rhymes with it.

   _____

Spelling Week 16 – Words with Long and Short *oo* Sounds

Say each word out loud. Look at the different letters that makethe long and short *oo* sounds. Copy and spell each word three times using colors of your choice.

1. wood _____ _____ _____

2. shook _____ _____ _____

3. grew _____ _____ _____

4. stood _____ _____ _____

5. true _____ _____ _____

6. food _____ _____ _____

7. chew _____ _____ _____

8. tooth _____ _____ _____

9. cookie _____ _____ _____

10. should _____ _____ _____

Spelling Tips

The long *oo* sound can be spelled with
- letters *ew* (*flew*) and *ue* (*blue*)
- letters *oo* (*food*)
- letters *ough* (*through*)

The short *oo* sound can be spelled with
- letters *oo* (*wool*)
- letters *ou* (*could*)

Spelling Week 16 – Words with Long and Short *oo* Sounds

| chew | cookie | food | grew | shook |
| stood | should | tooth | true | wood |

1. Fill in the blank using the best spelling word from the list.

   a) My little brother has a loose _____.

   b) She _____ in the window, staring at the rain falling.

   c) Most animals can smell _____ from far away.

   d) Dad and I baked a giant _____ for Mother's Day.

   e) Mom says to always _____ your food well.

   f) Our puppy _____ a lot in the past three months.

   g) I _____ clean my room before my friend comes over.

   h) Is it _____ that an elephant never forgets.

   i) Grandpa chopped _____ for the bonfire.

   j) During the earthquake, the whole house _____.

Brain Stretch

How many spelling words can you fit into one sentence and still make sense? Give it a try!

Spelling Week 16 – Word Study

1. Circle the words that have a long **oo** sound.

   a) menu   book   boot   flew   doe

   b) route   crow   fruit   wool   doom

   c) tissue   tool   sport   took   fool

   d) bloom   room   from   good   rule

2. Underline the words that have a short **oo** sound.

   a) spooky   look   pool   soot   flute

   b) tune   foot   stop   troops   shook

   c) coop   broom   good   book   loop

   d) zoom   wood   fool   cook   would

   e) soup   woof   group   should   groom

3. Write the correct letter beside the word.

   Write **S** for a short **oo** sound, **L** for a long **oo** sound, and **N** for neither sound.

   a) brook _____   b) putt _____   c) moon _____

   d) roof _____   e) grown _____   f) should _____

   g) sponge _____   h) crook _____   i) glue _____

Spelling Week 17 – Compound Words

Say each word out loud. Find the two small words that make the bigger word.

Copy and spell each word three times using colors of your choice.

1. baseball _____ _____ _____

2. snowman _____ _____ _____

3. firefly _____ _____ _____

4. cupcake _____ _____ _____

5. sunshine _____ _____ _____

6. popcorn _____ _____ _____

7. raindrop _____ _____ _____

8. doghouse _____ _____ _____

9. sailboat _____ _____ _____

10. backpack _____ _____ _____

Brain Stretch

- Create a word search puzzle based on the spelling words.
- On a piece of paper, write a sentence using each spelling word.

Spelling Week 17 – Compound Words

backpack **baseball** **cupcake** **doghouse** **firefly**
popcorn **raindrop** **sailboat** **snowman** **sunshine**

1. Fill in the blank using the best spelling word from the list.

   a) Dad painted Buster's _____ bright blue.

   b) Kayla put her books and pencils in her new _____.

   c) When we watch movies at home, my mom makes _____.

   d) Bill went to the lake and watched a big _____ go by.

   e) A _____ sat flashing its light on a rock in the forest.

   f) I love to get warmed up in the _____ in winter.

   g) A single _____ ran slowly down the window.

   h) Tammy joined the junior _____ team this spring.

   i) Last winter, we built the biggest _____ ever!

   j) Kerry chose a vanilla _____ for a special treat.

Brain Stretch

How many spelling words can you fit into one sentence and still make sense? Give it a try!

© Chalkboard Publishing Inc.

Spelling Week 17 – Word Study

Time for a fun puzzle! Look at the pieces to see how they match. The compound word on one side must match the same two words separated on the side facing it. Cut out all the puzzle pieces along the lines. Mix the pieces up well. Now, try to put the puzzle back together! Draw pictures on your puzzle pieces. **Hint: Not all words match up to other words.**

eyebrow	fingertip	hairpin	sunset
baseball / back + pack	backpack / butterfly	butter + fly / book + worm	bookworm / waterfall
fireman	dog + house	play + ground	flashlight
fire + man	doghouse	playground	flash + light
seashell / snow + man	snowman / door + bell	doorbell / afternoon	after + noon / teaspoon
sun + shine	fireworks	cross + walk	football
sunshine	fire + works	crosswalk	foot + ball
handshake / air + plane	airplane / hotdog	hot + dog / newspaper	news + paper / bookmark
toolbox	moonlight	homework	overhead

Spelling Week 18 – Words with *oi* and *oy*

Say each word out loud. Listen to the sounds *oi* and *oy* make.

Copy and spell each word three times using colors of your choice.

1. join _____ _____ _____

2. enjoy _____ _____ _____

3. loyal _____ _____ _____

4. boy _____ _____ _____

5. soil _____ _____ _____

6. noise _____ _____ _____

7. choice _____ _____ _____

8. annoy _____ _____ _____

9. coin _____ _____ _____

10. toy _____ _____ _____

Brain Stretch

- Create a word search puzzle based on the spelling words.
- On a piece of paper, write a sentence using each spelling word.

Spelling Week 18 – Words with *oi* and *oy*

| annoy | boy | choice | coin | enjoy |
| join | loyal | noise | soil | toy |

1. Fill in the blank using the best spelling word from the list.

   a) The dog ran in circles around the cat to _____ him.

   b) Diggers make a lot of _____ when they pull pavement up.

   c) Dad gave me the _____ of having pizza or a burger.

   d) The server brought our food and said, "_____ your meal."

   e) Uncle Joe's dog has been a _____ friend to him.

   f) The _____ rabbit I saw looked and felt like a live rabbit.

   g) Mom and I planted the seeds in good _____ in the garden.

   h) Niki wants to _____ the river clean-up crew.

   i) The _____ who knocked on the door was selling cookies.

   j) Alex found a _____ and put it in his piggy bank.

Brain Stretch

How many spelling words can you fit into one sentence and still make sense? Give it a try!

Spelling Week 18 – Word Study

1. Use the word list below to look for the words in the puzzle.

    Circle the word in the word search puzzle. Then cross out the word in the list.

S	P	O	I	L	B	A	X	A
O	E	I	D	L	M	N	O	V
Y	R	P	E	C	O	O	Z	O
U	K	J	C	F	I	I	Y	Y
H	W	R	O	U	S	S	O	A
A	H	O	Y	S	T	E	R	G
V	Q	Y	T	F	G	D	F	E
O	Y	A	C	O	I	L	I	H
I	S	L	A	I	K	M	B	J
D	R	F	T	L	Y	U	G	Z

| ahoy | avoid | coil | decoy | foil | moist |
| noise | oyster | royal | soy | spoil | voyage |

For these questions, rhyming words do not have to be spelled in the same way.

2. Write a word that rhymes with each word below.

   a) join _____   b) noise _____   c) choice _____

3. Write as many words as you can think of that end in the sound *oil*.

   _____

Spelling Week 19 – Words with an *s* Sound

Say each word out loud. Look at the different letters that make an **s** sound. Copy and spell each word three times using colors of your choice.

1. case
2. circle
3. silent
4. spice
5. cement
6. circus
7. cycle
8. since
9. city
10. space

Spelling Tip

The **s** sound can be spelled with letters **s**, **ce**, **ci**, and **cy**.

Spelling Week 19 – Words with an *s* Sound

case	cement	circle	circus	city
cycle	silent	since	space	spice

1. Fill in the blank using the best spelling word from the list.

   a) Jane wants to be an astronaut and travel to _____.

   b) At the _____, I like to watch the acrobats perform.

   c) It's been four days _____ we last had any sunshine.

   d) Detective Andrew was working on a very puzzling _____.

   e) Before a bad storm, birds often become very _____.

   f) A _____ can be the start of many interesting drawings.

   g) Aunt Deb makes _____ stepping stones for her yard.

   h) We live in the _____, and my cousins live in the country.

   i) Pepper is Jack's favorite _____.

   j) Rain, snow, and clouds are all part of the water _____.

Brain Stretch

How many spelling words can you fit into one sentence and still make sense? Give it a try!

© Chalkboard Publishing Inc.

Spelling Week 19 – Word Study

1. Each word is a thing or an object.

    Read the word out loud. Listen for the **s** sound.

    In the box, draw a picture of the thing or object.

horseshoe	**space**
cent	**sister**
bicycle	**spider**

Spelling Week 20 – Words with a *j* Sound

Say each word out loud. Look at the different letters that make a *j* sound.

Copy and spell each word three times using colors of your choice.

1. jump _____ _____ _____

2. jacket _____ _____ _____

3. gym _____ _____ _____

4. magic _____ _____ _____

5. gentle _____ _____ _____

6. huge _____ _____ _____

7. giant _____ _____ _____

8. large _____ _____ _____

9. joke _____ _____ _____

10. stage _____ _____ _____

Spelling Tip

The *j* sound can be spelled with the letters *j*, *ge*, *gy*, and *gi*.

Spelling Week 20 – Words with a *j* Sound

gentle	giant	gym	huge	jacket
joke	jump	large	magic	stage

1. Fill in the blank using the best spelling word from the list.

   a) Lynn finally had her chance to sing and perform on _____.

   b) The vet was very _____ with the sick animal.

   c) My class played basketball in the _____ on Tuesday.

   d) Our teacher read a fairy tale about a boy and a _____.

   e) My grandpa does _____ by pulling a coin out of my ear.

   f) A blue whale is such a _____ animal!

   g) When we added lemon juice to the tea, it turned _____.

   h) Hanna is laughing at the _____ book she is reading.

   i) Drinks come in small, medium, and _____ sizes.

   j) The sudden bang of the firecrackers made me _____!

Brain Stretch

How many spelling words can you fit into one sentence and still make sense? Give it a try!

Spelling Week 20 – Word Study

1. Write the name of the object in the picture on the line below.

    Put a checkmark (✓) in the box beside the names that have a *j* sound.

    Put an **X** in the box beside the names that don't have a *j* sound.

a) _____ ☐

b) _____ ☐

c) _____ ☐

d) _____ ☐

e) _____ ☐

f) _____ ☐

© Chalkboard Publishing Inc.

Spelling Week 21 – Words with *ow* and *ou*

Say each word out loud. Listen for the sounds **ow** and **ou** make.

Copy and spell each word three times using colors of your choice.

1. proud
2. pouch
3. frown
4. cloud
5. power
6. bounce
7. tower
8. hour
9. howl
10. crown

Brain Stretch

- Create a word search puzzle based on the spelling words.
- On a piece of paper, write a sentence using each spelling word.

Spelling Week 21 – Words with *ow* and *ou*

bounce	cloud	crown	frown	hour
howl	pouch	power	proud	tower

1. Fill in the blank using the best spelling word from the list.

   a) If you could have a super _____, what would it be?

   b) In the story, the princess was locked in a tall _____.

   c) A mother kangaroo has a _____ for carrying her baby.

   d) Queen Elizabeth has a golden _____ with many jewels.

   e) When I'm upset, I often _____.

   f) Marty's ball fell in a puddle, and now it won't _____..

   g) We saw a _____ that looked like an elephant.

   h) Jess practices piano for an _____ each day.

   i) At my aunt's cottage, we heard a wolf _____ at night.

   j) We are very _____ of our team for winning the game.

Brain Stretch

How many spelling words can you fit into one sentence and still make sense? Give it a try!

Spelling Week 21 – Word Study

Ask permission to use a magazine for this activity.

Cut out pictures to show the words below. Glue or tape them in place.

If you can't find a picture, you may make a drawing instead.

frown	cloud
crowd	sprout
pouch	tower

Spelling Week 22 – Months of the Year

Say each word out loud.

Copy and spell each word three times using colors of your choice.

1. January _____   _____

2. February _____   _____

3. March _____   _____

4. April _____   _____

5. May _____   _____

6. June _____   _____

7. July _____   _____

8. August _____   _____

9. September _____   _____

10. October _____   _____

11. November _____   _____

12. December _____   _____

© Chalkboard Publishing Inc.

Spelling Week 22 – Months of the Year

April	August	December	February
January	July	June	March
May	November	October	September

1. Fill in the blank using the best spelling word from the list.

   a) In _____, we celebrate the start of the new year.

   b) Students get a week-long break in _____.

   c) Christmas, Kwanzaa, and Hanukkah are celebrated in _____.

   d) In _____, school finishes for the summer.

   e) Canada Day is on the first day of _____.

   f) Queen Victoria's birthday is celebrated in _____.

   g) Valentine's Day is in _____.

   h) Easter is celebrated in _____.

   i) _____ is the last month before school starts.

   j) In _____, we celebrate Thanksgiving and Halloween.

   k) _____ is usually cold and snowy.

   l) In _____, students head back to school again.

Spelling Week 22 – Word Study

Each of the four seasons starts on a certain day of the year.

Write the season that goes with the picture below.

Write the month and date in which that season starts.

March 20   **September 23**   **June 21**   **December 22**

Season: _____

Starts: _____

Season: _____

Starts: _____

Season: _____

Starts: _____

Season: _____

Starts: _____

Spelling Week 23 – Consonant Digraphs *ch, sh, th,* and *wh*

Say each word out loud. Listen for the different sounds the digraphs make.

Copy and spell each word three times using colors of your choice.

1. cheese _____ _____ _____

2. teacher _____ _____ _____

3. shade _____ _____ _____

4. warmth _____ _____ _____

5. who _____ _____ _____

6. children _____ _____ _____

7. think _____ _____ _____

8. where _____ _____ _____

9. finish _____ _____ _____

10. these _____ _____ _____

Brain Stretch

- Create a word search puzzle based on the spelling words.
- On a piece of paper, write a sentence using each spelling word.

Spelling Week 23 – Consonant Digraphs *ch, sh, th,* and *wh*

cheese	children	finish	shade	teacher
these	think	warmth	where	who

1. Fill in the blank using the best spelling word from the list.

   a) The kittens snuggled up to their mother for _____.

   b) I could not see _____ was making all that noise!

   c) My dog Sparky loves to eat _____.

   d) Maria needs a quiet place to _____ when she studies.

   e) My mother will love _____ plants!

   f) Our _____ showed us how to make paper flowers.

   g) Tim could not remember _____ he left his pen.

   h) Sara was sure she would _____ the race this time.

   i) This big maple tree provides cool _____ in summer.

   j) The _____ in my class love to paint and draw.

Brain Stretch

How many spelling words can you fit into one sentence and still make sense? Give it a try!

Spelling Week 23 – Word Study

1. Write the correct digraph letters in the word. Use **ch**, **sh**, **th**, or **wh**.
   Say the word out loud to check.

   a) _____en b) _____under c) _____ingles d) pin_____

   e) wi_____ f) _____icken g) fif_____ h) _____eap

   i) _____immer j) _____isper k) _____ing l) spla_____

2. How many words can you make? Use only **ch, sh, th,** and **wh** and the letters given to make the words. Write your words on the line.

   Examples: am   wham   sham

   a) ip _____

   b) ick _____

   c) wi _____

   d) at _____

   e) en _____

   f) in _____

   g) eat _____

   h) ose _____

Spelling Week 24 – Consonant Blends *scr, spl, spr,* and *str*

Say each word out loud. Listen to the sounds each consonant blend makes.

Copy and spell each word three times using colors of your choice.

1. stream _____ _____ _____

2. scratch _____ _____ _____

3. split _____ _____ _____

4. strong _____ _____ _____

5. splash _____ _____ _____

6. spring _____ _____ _____

7. spray _____ _____ _____

8. strip _____ _____ _____

9. scrape _____ _____ _____

10. strange _____ _____ _____

Brain Stretch

- Create a word search puzzle based on the spelling words.
- On a piece of paper, write a sentence using each spelling word.

Spelling Week 24 – Consonant Blends *scr*, *spl*, *spr*, and *str*

scrape	scratch	split	splash	spray
spring	strange	stream	strip	strong

1. Fill in the blank using the best spelling word from the list.

   a) We _____ Mom's air plants with water every three days.

   b) There's a very _____ bug sitting on that plant.

   c) When the alarm bell rings, the firemen _____ into action.

   d) My brother's fish flicks its tail to make a big _____.

   e) Dad helped us to _____ the apple in half.

   f) I got a _____ on my arm from that tree branch.

   g) If you run on the sidewalk, you might fall and _____ your knee.

   h) Cam added another _____ of paper to the paper chain.

   i) We saw frogs and minnows in the _____ by our house.

   j) My uncle is very _____ and can lift us easily.

Brain Stretch

How many spelling words can you fit into one sentence and still make sense? Give it a try!

Spelling Week 24 – Word Study

Write a short story using as many of these new words as you can.

screen	**scribble**	**splatter**	**splinter**	**sprinkle**
sprint	**stray**	**string**	**stripe**	**strong**

_____

_____

_____

_____

_____

_____

_____

_____

_____

Spelling Week 25 – Easily Misspelled Words

Some words can be easily misspelled because of how they sound when you say them.

Say each word out loud. Listen to how the words are pronounced.

Copy and spell each word three times using colors of your choice.

1. again _____ _____ _____

2. until _____ _____ _____

3. many _____ _____ _____

4. friend _____ _____ _____

5. people _____ _____ _____

6. learn _____ _____ _____

7. thought _____ _____ _____

8. another _____ _____ _____

9. always _____ _____ _____

10. school _____ _____ _____

Brain Stretch

- Create a word search puzzle based on the spelling words.
- On a piece of paper, write a sentence using each spelling word.

Spelling Week 25 – Easily Misspelled Words

| again | always | another | friend | learn |
| many | people | school | thought | until |

1. Fill in the blank using the best spelling word from the list.

   a) Andrew loves learning new things at _____.

   b) Some very excited _____ came to see our new puppies.

   c) Look! _____ flower is blooming in my garden!

   d) Mom _____ plays her favorite music when she is cooking.

   e) I have to wait _____ Friday to open my present.

   f) I _____ I heard my mother call me, so I have to go home.

   g) Grandpa is taking a class so he can _____ to paint.

   h) Our cat snuck out the front door _____ when I opened it.

   i) There are _____ mosquitoes flying near those bushes.

   j) Matt is a very good _____ to my Uncle Sam.

Brain Stretch

How many spelling words can you fit into one sentence and still make sense? Give it a try!

Spelling Week 25 – Word Study

Ask permission to use a magazine or newspaper for this activity.

Cut out letters to spell the word below.

Glue or tape the letters in order on the line.

friend	**learn**
always	**people**
school	**until**
again	**many**

Spelling Week 26 – R-controlled Vowels with *or, er, ir, ur,* and *ear*

> When the letter **r** follows a vowel, it changes the sound of the vowel.
>
> *Examples:* cat car   box born   gift girl

Say each word out loud. Listen to how the vowels are pronounced.

Copy and spell each word three times using colors of your choice.

1. girl
2. burn
3. here
4. were
5. fear
6. wear
7. bird
8. world
9. turn
10. fork

Spelling Week 26 – R-controlled Vowels with *or, er, ir, ur,* and *ear*

bird	burn	fear	fork	girl
here	turn	wear	were	world

1. Fill in the blank using the best spelling word from the list.

   a) Peter wants to travel all over and see the whole _____.

   b) Sandy has a _____ of heights.

   c) That _____ has beautiful, curly red hair.

   d) Mike wants to _____ a superhero costume on Halloween.

   e) I have to fill up my _____ feeder today.

   f) My cousin Jane will _____ seven this weekend.

   g) Grandpa says things _____ different when he was young.

   h) You should flip the pancakes now so they won't _____.

   i) My baby sister uses a spoon instead of a _____.

   j) To play this game, we have to all line up _____.

Brain Stretch

How many spelling words can you fit into one sentence and still make sense? Give it a try!

Spelling Week 26 – Word Study

1. How many letter combinations can you think of that make an **er** sound?
   _____

2. a) Write as many words as you can that have the letters **ear**.
   _____

   b) How many different sounds do those letters have? _____

3. You are going to decode a secret message! The letters of the alphabet are each represented by a number, as shown below.

1	2	3	4	5	6	7	8	9	10	11	12	13
A	B	C	D	E	F	G	H	I	J	K	L	M

14	15	16	17	18	19	20	21	22	23	24	25	26
N	O	P	Q	R	S	T	U	V	W	X	Y	Z

Write the letter on the line above the number to decode the message.

a) __ __ __ __ __ __ __ __ / __ __ __ / __ __ __ __ __ __ __ __
   12 5 1 18 14 9 14 7   14 5 23   19 16 5 12 12 9 14 7

   __ __ __ __ __ / __ __ / __ __ __!
   23 15 18 4 19   9 19   6 21 14

b) __ __ __ __ / __ / __ __ __ __ __ / __ __ __ / __ __ __ __ __ '
   7 9 22 5   1   19 13 9 12 5   1 14 4   25 15 21 12 12

   __ __ __ / __ __ __ / __ __ __ __.
   7 5 20   15 14 5   2 1 3 11

Spelling Week 27 – R-controlled Vowels with *ar, are, or,* and *ore*

The letters *or* and *ore* make the same sound.

Examples: for wore store

The letters *ar* and *are* sound different. The *r* changes the way the vowel sounds.

Examples: far tar care share

Say each word out loud. Listen to the sound of the vowels before the *r*.

Copy and spell each word three times using colors of your choice.

1. park _____ _____ _____

2. fork _____ _____ _____

3. more _____ _____ _____

4. fare _____ _____ _____

5. sport _____ _____ _____

6. aren't _____ _____ _____

7. shore _____ _____ _____

8. normal _____ _____ _____

9. bored _____ _____ _____

10. harm _____ _____ _____

Spelling Week 27 – R-controlled Vowels with *ar, are, or,* and *ore*

aren't	bored	fare	fork	harm
more	normal	park	shore	sport

1. Fill in the blank using the best spelling word from the list.

   a) Soccer is my family's favorite _____.

   b) This summer is much hotter than _____.

   c) I have just enough money to pay for bus _____.

   d) Every summer, we search for shells on the _____.

   e) _____ you coming to the library with us today?

   f) Our dog is huge, but he would never _____ small animals.

   g) I draw, paint, or read a book whenever I'm _____.

   h) Mary likes to twirl her spaghetti on her _____.

   i) My friend's dog Bo loves to play frisbee at the _____.

   j) When my Aunt Amy laughs, she makes me laugh even _____.

Brain Stretch

How many spelling words can you fit into one sentence and still make sense? Give it a try!

Spelling Week 27 – Word Study

1. On the lines below, write these 6 words in alphabetical order.

   pork   **spark**   **bored**   **floor**   **apart**   **hare**

   a) _____   b) _____   c) _____

   d) _____   e) _____   f) _____

2. Write a short sentence using the word below. Check your punctation.

   a) care _____

   b) tore _____

   c) shark _____

   d) morning _____

   e) large _____

   f) stare _____

   g) before _____

   h) short _____

   i) space _____

Spelling Week 28 – Words with an *f* Sound Spelled *ph*, *gh*, and *f*

Say each word out loud. Listen to the *f* sound the different letters make.

Copy and spell each word three times using colors of your choice.

1. photo
2. rough
3. Friday
4. laugh
5. favorite
6. forget
7. cough
8. graph
9. phone
10. father

Brain Stretch

- Create a word search puzzle based on the spelling words.
- On a piece of paper, write a sentence using each spelling word.

Spelling Week 28 – Words with an *f* Sound Spelled *ph, gh,* and *f*

cough	father	favorite	forget	Friday
graph	laugh	phone	photo	rough

1. Fill in the blank using the best spelling word from the list.

   a) Orange is Marco's _____ color.

   b) Kim stayed home from school with a bad cold and _____.

   c) In math, we made a _____ of people's favorite animals.

   d) I must not _____ to take my project to school tomorrow.

   e) My cat's tongue is very _____ on my skin.

   f) Cindy's _____ is a great wood carver.

   g) We use the _____ to call our grandparents every weekend.

   h) _____ is the last day of the school week.

   i) My sister took a beautiful _____ of a flower in the garden.

   j) The funny look on that dog's face makes me _____.

Brain Stretch

How many spelling words can you fit into one sentence and still make sense? Give it a try!

Spelling Week 28 – Word Study

1. Write a short definition for the word below. Explain it in your own words.

   a) favorite _____

   b) forget _____

   c) rough _____

2. A **synonym** is a word that means the same as another word.

   Circle the synonym for the bolded word.

   a) **laugh**   upset   giggle   b) **rough**   bumpy   sneaky

   c) **photo**   drawing   picture   d) **father**   uncle   daddy

3. An **antonym** is a word that has the opposite meaning of another word.

   Circle the antonym for the bolded word.

   a) **rough**   smooth   shiny   b) **forget**   memory   remember

   c) **laugh**   cry   angry   d) **favorite** dull   disliked

4. Write as many words as you can that rhyme with the word below.

   a) rough _____

   b) laugh _____

© Chalkboard Publishing Inc.

Spelling Week 29 – Words with Silent Letters

Say each word out loud. Pay attention to which letters you can't hear.

Copy and spell each word three times using colors of your choice.

1. honest _____ _____ _____

2. knife _____ _____ _____

3. climb _____ _____ _____

4. ghost _____ _____ _____

5. scent _____ _____ _____

6. write _____ _____ _____

7. sign _____ _____ _____

8. chalk _____ _____ _____

9. guest _____ _____ _____

10. calm _____ _____ _____

Brain Stretch

- Create a word search puzzle based on the spelling words.
- On a piece of paper, write a sentence using each spelling word.

Spelling Week 29 – Words with Silent Letters

calm	chalk	climb	ghost	guest
honest	knife	scent	sign	write

1. Fill in the blank using the best spelling word from the list.

   a) My father used a sharp _____ to cut the watermelon.

   b) Cassie dressed up as a _____ for Halloween.

   c) My brother and I always _____ on the jungle gym at the park.

   d) We all wait at the stop _____ for the crossing guard.

   e) In class today, we learned to _____ all the alphabet letters.

   f) The leaves are not moving because the air is _____.

   g) I found her book and I gave it back because I am _____.

   h) My favorite _____ is lilac flowers.

   i) We used colorful _____ to draw pictures on our driveway.

   j) A hungry squirrel was a surprise _____ at our backyard party.

Brain Stretch

How many spelling words can you fit into one sentence and still make sense? Give it a try!

Spelling Week 29 – Word Study

You already learned about words with silent *e*.

There many more silent letters, as you will see below.

1. Say the word out loud. Underline the letter or letters you can't hear.

    Hint: Some words have more than one silent letter.

    a) knight   b) school   c) comb   d) calf

    e) thumb   f) phone   g) salmon   h) doubt

    i) knock   j) honour   k) airplane   l) crumb

    m) rhyme   n) scissors   o) muscle   p) gnome

2. Write all the words from Question 1 that have a silent *b*.

    _____

3. Write all the words from Question 1 that have a silent *e*.

    _____

4. Fill in the missing silent letter.

    a) sal_____   b) _____rong   c) _____not   d) lam_____

    e) _____nome   f) wa_____k   g) li_____ht   h) cran_____

Spelling Week 30 – Homophones

Say each word out loud. Listen for the words that sound the same.

Copy and spell each word three times using colors of your choice.

1. which _____ _____ _____

2. knight _____ _____ _____

3. where _____ _____ _____

4. here _____ _____ _____

5. night _____ _____ _____

6. write _____ _____ _____

7. witch _____ _____ _____

8. hear _____ _____ _____

9. wear _____ _____ _____

10. right _____ _____ _____

Brain Stretch

- Create a word search puzzle based on the spelling words.
- On a piece of paper, write a sentence using each spelling word.

Spelling Week 30 – Homophones

hear	here	knight	night	right
wear	where	which	witch	write

1. Fill in the blank using the best spelling word from the list.

   a) The mean _____ turned the prince into a toad.

   b) My grandmother is going to stay _____ this weekend.

   c) The brave _____ wasn't afraid of the fire-breathing dragon.

   d) In class, we all had to _____ about our summer holidays

   e) I like to _____ my cat purring when she's happy.

   f) Cam will _____ his new suit to the wedding.

   g) _____ color should we paint my bedroom—blue or green?

   h) My grandpa can't remember _____ he left his glasses.

   i) I am left handed, but my sister is _____ handed.

   j) Many people like to go outside to watch the stars at _____.

Brain Stretch

How many spelling words can you fit into one sentence and still make sense? Give it a try!

Spelling Week 30 – Word Study

1. Draw a line from the word in the left column to its homophone in the right column.

   a) hair   pale

   b) hear   reel

   c) stare   reed

   d) their   hare

   e) pail   stair

   f) real   here

   g) read   there

2. Circle the word that goes with the definition.

   a) **hair hare**   type of large rabbit with long ears

   b) **stare stair**   look at someone or something for a long time

   c) **pale pail**   very light in color

   d) **sale sail**   part of a ship that catches the wind to help the ship move

   e) **real reel**   cylinder on which film, thread, or wire can be wound

   f) **reed read**   tall, grass plant that grows in water or marshes

   g) **heel heal**   become healthy again

Spelling Week 1 – Test

Name: _____

Listen to the spelling words. Print each spelling word.

1. _____
2. _____
3. _____
4. _____
5. _____

6. _____
7. _____
8. _____
9. _____
10. _____

Bonus

1. _____
2. _____

Spelling Week 2 – Test

Name: _____

Listen to the spelling words. Print each spelling word.

1. _____
2. _____
3. _____
4. _____
5. _____

6. _____
7. _____
8. _____
9. _____
10. _____

Bonus

1. _____
2. _____

Spelling Week 3 – Test

Name: _____

Listen to the spelling words. Print each spelling word.

1. _____
2. _____
3. _____
4. _____
5. _____

6. _____
7. _____
8. _____
9. _____
10. _____

Bonus

1. _____
2. _____

Spelling Week 4 – Test

Name: _____

Listen to the spelling words. Print each spelling word.

1. _____
2. _____
3. _____
4. _____
5. _____

6. _____
7. _____
8. _____
9. _____
10. _____

Bonus

1. _____
2. _____

Spelling Week 5 – Test

Name: _____

Listen to the spelling words. Print each spelling word.

1. _____
2. _____
3. _____
4. _____
5. _____

6. _____
7. _____
8. _____
9. _____
10. _____

Bonus

1. _____
2. _____

Spelling Week 6 – Test

Name: _____

Listen to the spelling words. Print each spelling word.

1. _____
2. _____
3. _____
4. _____
5. _____

6. _____
7. _____
8. _____
9. _____
10. _____

Bonus

1. _____
2. _____

Spelling Week 7 – Test

Name: _____

Listen to the spelling words. Print each spelling word.

1. _____   6. _____

2. _____   7. _____

3. _____   8. _____

4. _____   9. _____

5. _____   10. _____

Bonus

1. _____   2. _____

Spelling Week 8 – Test

Name: _____

Listen to the spelling words. Print each spelling word.

1. _____   6. _____

2. _____   7. _____

3. _____   8. _____

4. _____   9. _____

5. _____   10. _____

Bonus

1. _____   2. _____

Spelling Week 9 – Test

Name: _____

Listen to the spelling words. Print each spelling word.

1. _____   6. _____

2. _____   7. _____

3. _____   8. _____

4. _____   9. _____

5. _____   10. _____

Bonus

1. _____   2. _____

- -

Spelling Week 10 – Test

Name: _____

Listen to the spelling words. Print each spelling word.

1. _____   6. _____

2. _____   7. _____

3. _____   8. _____

4. _____   9. _____

5. _____   10. _____

Bonus

1. _____   2. _____

Spelling Week 11 – Test   Name: _____

Listen to the spelling words. Print each spelling word.

1. _____   6. _____

2. _____   7. _____

3. _____   8. _____

4. _____   9. _____

5. _____   10. _____

Bonus

1. _____   2. _____

Spelling Week 12 – Test   Name: _____

Listen to the spelling words. Print each spelling word.

1. _____   6. _____

2. _____   7. _____

3. _____   8. _____

4. _____   9. _____

5. _____   10. _____

Bonus

1. _____   2. _____

Spelling Week 13 – Test

Name: _____

Listen to the spelling words. Print each spelling word.

1. _____   6. _____

2. _____   7. _____

3. _____   8. _____

4. _____   9. _____

5. _____   10. _____

Bonus

1. _____   2. _____

Spelling Week 14 – Test

Name: _____

Listen to the spelling words. Print each spelling word.

1. _____   6. _____

2. _____   7. _____

3. _____   8. _____

4. _____   9. _____

5. _____   10. _____

Bonus

1. _____   2. _____

Spelling Week 15 – Test   Name: _____

Listen to the spelling words. Print each spelling word.

1. _____   6. _____

2. _____   7. _____

3. _____   8. _____

4. _____   9. _____

5. _____   10. _____

Bonus

1. _____   2. _____

Spelling Week 16 – Test   Name: _____

Listen to the spelling words. Print each spelling word.

1. _____   6. _____

2. _____   7. _____

3. _____   8. _____

4. _____   9. _____

5. _____   10. _____

Bonus

1. _____   2. _____

Spelling Week 17 – Test

Name: _____

Listen to the spelling words. Print each spelling word.

1. _____ 6. _____

2. _____ 7. _____

3. _____ 8. _____

4. _____ 9. _____

5. _____ 10. _____

Bonus

1. _____ 2. _____

Spelling Week 18 – Test

Name: _____

Listen to the spelling words. Print each spelling word.

1. _____ 6. _____

2. _____ 7. _____

3. _____ 8. _____

4. _____ 9. _____

5. _____ 10. _____

Bonus

1. _____ 2. _____

Spelling Week 19 – Test   Name: _____

Listen to the spelling words. Print each spelling word.

1. _____   6. _____

2. _____   7. _____

3. _____   8. _____

4. _____   9. _____

5. _____   10. _____

Bonus

1. _____   2. _____

Spelling Week 20 – Test   Name: _____

Listen to the spelling words. Print each spelling word.

1. _____   6. _____

2. _____   7. _____

3. _____   8. _____

4. _____   9. _____

5. _____   10. _____

Bonus

1. _____   2. _____

Spelling Week 21 – Test   Name: _____

Listen to the spelling words. Print each spelling word.

1. _____   6. _____

2. _____   7. _____

3. _____   8. _____

4. _____   9. _____

5. _____   10. _____

Bonus

1. _____   2. _____

Spelling Week 22 – Test   Name: _____

Listen to the spelling words. Print each spelling word.

1. _____   7. _____

2. _____   8. _____

3. _____   9. _____

4. _____   10. _____

5. _____   11. _____

6. _____   12. _____

Spelling Week 23 – Test   Name: _____

Listen to the spelling words. Print each spelling word.

1. _____   6. _____

2. _____   7. _____

3. _____   8. _____

4. _____   9. _____

5. _____   10. _____

Bonus

1. _____   2. _____

Spelling Week 24 – Test   Name: _____

Listen to the spelling words. Print each spelling word.

1. _____   6. _____

2. _____   7. _____

3. _____   8. _____

4. _____   9. _____

5. _____   10. _____

Bonus

1. _____   2. _____

Spelling Week 25 – Test

Name: _____

Listen to the spelling words. Print each spelling word.

1. _____   6. _____

2. _____   7. _____

3. _____   8. _____

4. _____   9. _____

5. _____   10. _____

Bonus

1. _____   2. _____

Spelling Week 26 – Test

Name: _____

Listen to the spelling words. Print each spelling word.

1. _____   6. _____

2. _____   7. _____

3. _____   8. _____

4. _____   9. _____

5. _____   10. _____

Bonus

1. _____   2. _____

Spelling Week 27 – Test   Name: _____

Listen to the spelling words. Print each spelling word.

1. _____   6. _____

2. _____   7. _____

3. _____   8. _____

4. _____   9. _____

5. _____   10. _____

Bonus

1. _____   2. _____

Spelling Week 28 – Test   Name: _____

Listen to the spelling words. Print each spelling word.

1. _____   6. _____

2. _____   7. _____

3. _____   8. _____

4. _____   9. _____

5. _____   10. _____

Bonus

1. _____   2. _____

Spelling Week 29 – Test

Name: _____

Listen to the spelling words. Print each spelling word.

1. _____   6. _____

2. _____   7. _____

3. _____   8. _____

4. _____   9. _____

5. _____   10. _____

Bonus

1. _____   2. _____

Spelling Week 30 – Test

Name: _____

Listen to the spelling words. Print each spelling word.

1. _____   6. _____

2. _____   7. _____

3. _____   8. _____

4. _____   9. _____

5. _____   10. _____

Bonus

1. _____   2. _____

Everyday Words to Know How to Spell

The Fry word list contains the most common words used in English listed in order of frequency and includes all parts of speech.

the	or	will	number
of	one	up	no
and	had	other	way
a	by	about	could
to	words	out	people
in	but	many	my
is	not	then	than
you	what	them	first
that	all	these	water
it	were	so	been
he	we	some	called
was	when	her	who
for	your	would	oil
on	can	make	sit
are	said	like	now
as	there	him	find
with	use	into	long
his	an	time	down
they	each	has	day
I	which	look	did
at	she	two	get
be	do	more	come
this	how	write	made
have	their	go	may
from	if	see	part

Everyday Words to Know How to Spell

The Fry word list contains the most common words used in English listed in order of frequency and includes all parts of speech.

over	say	set	try
new	great	put	kind
sound	where	end	hand
take	help	does	picture
only	through	another	again
little	much	well	change
work	before	large	off
know	line	must	play
place	right	big	spell
years	too	even	air
live	means	such	away
me	old	because	animal
back	any	turn	house
give	same	here	point
most	tell	why	page
very	boy	ask	letter
after	follow	went	mother
things	came	men	answer
our	want	read	found
just	show	need	study
name	also	land	still
good	around	different	learn
sentence	form	home	should
man	three	us	world
think	small	move	

Everyday Words to Know How to Spell

The Fry word list contains the most common words used in English listed in order of frequency and includes all parts of speech.

high	saw	important	miss
every	left	until	idea
near	don't	children	enough
add	few	side	eat
food	while	feet	face
between	along	car	watch
own	might	mile	far
below	close	night	real
country	something	walk	almost
plant	seem	white	let
last	next	sea	above
school	hard	began	girl
father	open	grow	sometimes
keep	example	took	mountains
tree	begin	river	cut
never	life	four	young
start	always	carry	talk
city	those	state	soon
earth	both	once	list
eyes	paper	book	song
light	together	hear	being
thought	got	stop	leave
head	group	without	family
under	often	second	it's
story	run	late	

Spelling Practice Menu

Color Code Write out your spelling words using one color for the vowels and another color for the consonants.	**Rainbow Words** Write out your spelling words into the shape of a rainbow using the colors of the rainbow.	**Hidden Words** Draw a picture outline. Add your spelling words to the picture so that they are "hiding." Color your picture.
Cut it out! Cut letters out of a magazine. Spell out your words and glue them onto a sheet of paper.	**Word Search** Create a word search based on your spelling words.	**Rhyming Words** Write out your spelling words with a rhyming word next to each of them.
Alphabetical Order Print your spelling words in alphabetical order.	**Spelling Word Typing** Type your spelling words on a computer or other device.	**Magnetic Letter Words** Use magnetic letters to make your spelling words.
Spelling Race How many times can you write out your spelling words in three minutes?	**Sort It Out** Sort your spelling words into categories of your choice and record on a piece of paper.	**Spelling Word Fun** Form your spelling words using: • modelling clay • pipe cleaners • toothpicks

_____'s Word Search

Create a word search and share it with someone.

Word List

Spelling Tracker

Name	Week ___	Week ___	Week ___	Week ___	Week ___	Week ___	Week ___	Week ___	Week ___	Week ___	Week ___	Week ___	Week ___	Week ___

Answers

Spelling Week 1 – Words with a Short *a* Sound, pp. 2–3
1. a) apple b) brand c) catch d) away e) about f) class g) than h) after i) stand j) ask

Spelling Week 1 – Word Study, p. 4
1. a) houses b) lashes c) passes d) batches e) flashes f) glasses g) boxes h) trucks i) peaches
2. a) 3 syllables b) 1 syllable c) 4 syllables
3. leave a vehicle in a spot

Spelling Week 2 – Words with a Short *e* Sound, pp. 5–6
1. a) best b) said c) help d) Next e) friend f) vent g) test h) forget i) else j) dress

Spelling Week 2 – Word Study, p. 7
1. a) letter b) spread c) sled d) lend e) said
2. a) went b) best c) fed d) crest
3. Sample answers: When summer comes, my dog starts to shed hair. My father stores his garden tools in the shed in our yard.

Spelling Week 3 – Words with a Short *i* Sound, pp. 8–9
1. a) children b) little c) pick d) slip e) This f) think g) its h) drink i) if j) itch

Spelling Week 3 – Word Study, p. 10
1. a) families b) fifties c) cities d) giveaways e) piggies f) displays g) hippies h) stories i) memories
2. a) 2 syllables b) 5 syllables c) 1 syllable
3. Sample answers: The baseball player was up at bat. The bat was as black as the night.

Spelling Week 4 – Words with a Short *o* Sound, pp. 11–12
1. a) rot b) rock c) pond d) spot e) shop f) hot g) body h) drop i) odd j) lots

Spelling Week 4 – Word Study, p. 13
1. a) boxes b) porches c) mosses d) torches e) bosses f) sloshes g) glosses h) sandboxes i) shashes
2. Sample answers: hot, pot, lot, spot, shot, got, taught, fought, caught
3. Sample answers: I went to the science fair. It is only fair to share the cookies with everyone.

Spelling Week 5 – Words with a Short *u* Sound, pp. 14–15
1. a) buzz b) stuffing c) mother d) under e) cut f) munch g) summer h) month i) Monday j) lunch

Spelling Week 5 – Word Study, p. 16
1. a) couch, through b) ground, bounce c) pout, beauty d) grouch, guest e) cove, about
2. a) butter b) cover c) glove d) rough e) fudge f) fluff g) stump h) touch i) double

Answers

Spelling Week 6 – Words with a Long *a* Sound, pp. 17–18
1. a) sway b) paint c) play d) lake e) tale f) came g) snail h) mail i) save j) today

Spelling Week 6 – Word Study, p. 19
1. a) break, late, bait b) face, lazy, state c) paste, grate, case d) play, made, sway e) clay, gate, eight
2. A, J, K
3. 8, 18, 28, 38, 48, 58, 68, 78, 80, 81, 82, 83, 84, 85, 86, 87, 88, 89, 98

Spelling Week 7 – Words with a Long *e* Sound, pp. 20–21
1. a) easy b) street c) sweet d) treat e) These f) team g) speed h) please i) each j) theme

Spelling Week 7 – Word Study, p. 22
1. a) stories b) puppies c) carries d) hurries e) babies f) berries g) families h) parties i) daises
2. a) 2 syllables b) 1 syllable c) 3 syllables
3. Ontario
4. evergreen, babysitter, jellybean

Spelling Week 8 – Words with a Long *i* Sound, pp. 23–24
1. a) twice b) night c) spice d) spy e) high f) dry g) tie h) fine i) like j) pile

Spelling Week 8 – Word Study, p. 25
1. a) spine, sign, guy, fly b) kind, iron, hind c) rise, eye, d) twine, mine, twice, white e) grind, wipe
2. a) okay b) sneaky
3. a) yours b) lose
4. five, nine
5. Sample answers: live, drive, dive, survive, arrive; mine, line, spine, fine, dine, wine, whine, shine

Spelling Week 9 – Words with a Long *o* Sound, pp. 26–27
1. a) both b) almost c) grow d) gold e) bone f) alone g) coat h) show i) load j) coach

Answers

Spelling Week 9 – Word Study, p. 28
1. <u>Mario</u> and his family took a trip to the zoo. <u>Most</u> of them were excited to see all the animals. But his cousin <u>Lori</u> didn't want to <u>go</u>. She was afraid of the <u>hippos</u> and <u>polar</u> bears. Her cousin <u>Tony</u> held her hand and <u>told</u> her about each animal as they went. There was <u>so</u> much to learn! When she saw the <u>hippos</u> <u>rolling</u> in the water, she started to laugh. The <u>hippos</u> were having fun! The <u>polar</u> bears were playing with a ball. They were having fun, too! One <u>old</u> bear was sleeping. <u>Lori</u> and her family were safe behind walls the <u>whole</u> time. When they left the zoo, <u>Lori</u> said she couldn't wait to <u>go</u> to the zoo again!
2. a) score b) run
3. a) wide b) sink
4. a) 3 syllables b) 2 syllables c) 1 syllable
5. a type of blanket

Spelling Week 10 – Words with a Long *u* Sound, pp. 29–30
1. a) cube b) unicorn c) cute d) argue e) fuse f) chew g) Pure h) value i) huge j) use

Spelling Week 10 – Word Study, p. 31
1. a) argue b) ewe c) cube d) true e) few f) rescue

Spelling Week 11 – Words with *y* as Long *i* and Long *e* Sounds, pp. 32–33
1. a) sunny b) why c) cry d) jelly e) very f) fly g) dry h) family i) story j) shy

Spelling Week 11 – Word Study, p. 34
1. a) itchy b) family c) fry d) sky e) angry f) sticky
2. a) butter + fly, fry + pan b) dragon + fly, jelly + bean c) eye + ball, sky + line

Spelling Week 12 – Contractions, pp. 35–36
1. a) you'll b) we're c) We've d) I'd e) there's f) wouldn't g) that's h) didn't i) isn't j) He's

Spelling Week 12 – Word Study, p. 37
1. a) circle "willn't"; won't b) circle "W'ere"; We're c) circle "Iam"; I'm d) circle "Iti's"; It's e) circle "h'es"; he's
2. a) could not b) has not c) we are d) she is e) that is f) cannot g) is not h) will not i) you will j) did not

Spelling Week 13 – Double Consonants, pp. 38–39
1. a) zipper b) better c) stuff d) dinner e) funny f) happen g) buzzer h) soccer i) full j) miss

Spelling Week 13 – Word Study, p. 40
1. a) chopped, chopping b) knitted, knitting c) dragged, dragging d) skidded, skidding e) rubbed, rubbing
2. a) tripped, calling b) stopping, smelling c) slipped, missing d) chopped

Answers

Spelling Week 14 – Words That End in Double Consonants, pp. 41–42
1. a) hiss b) press c) grass d) fluff e) jazz f) bull g) cliff h) spill i) wall j) doll

Spelling Week 14 – Word Study, p. 43
1. Sample answers: a) well, sell, tell, gel, fell, swell, spell b) gas, bass, sass, pass, class, glass, grass, crass, brass c) cuff, buff, muff, fluff, stuff, rough, tough, enough d) wall, call, fall, all, tall, gall, doll, crawl, brawl e) bull, wool, full f) ill, fill, bill, till, mill, will, pill, sill, trill, frill, still, krill, skill, spill, swill g) boss, moss, floss, toss, loss h) sole, pole, vole, role, mole, troll, foal, goal, poll, toll, bowl, soul
2. a) healthy b) fill
3. a) empty b) short

Spelling Week 15 – Words That End in Silent e, pp. 44–45
1. a) file b) dive c) phone d) store e) shave f) cute g) save h) here i) line j) like

Spelling Week 15 – Word Study, p. 46
1. a) skated, skating b) smiled, smiling c) danced, dancing d) hoped, hoping e) saved, saving f) joked, joking g) waved, waving
2. one, five, nine
3. Sample answers: one: fun, run, sun, ton; five: live, dive, alive, drive, arrive, thrive; nine: fine, mine, line, wine, sign, swine

Spelling Week 16 – Words with Long and Short oo Sounds, pp. 47–48
1. a) tooth b) stood c) food d) cookie e) chew f) grew g) should h) true i) wood j) shook

Spelling Week 16 – Word Study, p. 49
1. a) menu, boot, flew b) route, fruit, doom c) tissue, tool, fool d) bloom, room, rule
2. a) look, soot b) foot, shook c) good, book d) would, cook e) woof, should
3. a) S b) N c) L d) L e) N f) S g) N h) S i) L

Spelling Week 17 – Compound Words, pp. 50–51
1. a) doghouse b) backpack c) popcorn d) sailboat e) firefly f) sunshine g) raindrop h) baseball i) snowman j) cupcake

Spelling Week 17 – Word Study, p. 52
You may wish to walk around the room and check that children have matched up the puzzle pieces correctly.

Spelling Week 18 – Words with *oi* and *oy*, pp. 53–54
1. a) annoy b) noise c) Enjoy d) loyal e) toy f) soil g) join h) boy i) coin j) choice

Answers

Spelling Week 18 – Word Study, p. 55

1.

S	P	O	I	L	B	A	X	A
O	E	I	D	L	M	N	O	V
Y	R	P	E	C	O	O	Z	O
U	K	J	C	F	I	I	Y	Y
H	W	R	O	U	S	S	O	A
A	H	O	Y	S	T	E	R	G
V	Q	Y	T	F	G	D	F	E
O	Y	A	C	O	I	L	I	H
I	S	L	A	I	K	M	B	J
D	R	F	T	L	Y	U	G	Z

2. Sample answers: a) coin b) boys, toys c) voice
3. Sample answers: coil, foil, boil, soil, royal, loyal, spoil

Spelling Week 19 – Words with an *s* Sound, pp. 56–57
1. a) space b) circus c) since d) case e) silent f) circle g) cement h) city i) spice j) cycle

Spelling Week 19 – Word Study, p. 58
1. You might wish to create a bulletin board display of children's drawings.

Spelling Week 20 – Words with a *j* Sound, pp. 59–60
1. a) stage b) gentle c) gym d) giant e) magic f) huge g) blue h) joke i) large j) jump

Spelling Week 20 – Word Study, p. 61
1. a) cow, ✘ b) giant, ✔ c) jacket, ✔ d) grapes, ✘ e) magic, ✔ f) jump, ✔

Spelling Week 21 – Words with *ow* and *ou*, pp. 62–63
1. a) power b) tower c) pouch d) crown e) frown f) bounce g) cloud h) hour i) howl. j) proud
You may wish to ask volunteers to share with the class what super power they would have and why they would have it.

Spelling Week 21 – Word Study, p. 64
You may wish to create a bulletin board display of children's pages.

Spelling Week 22 – Months of the Year, pp. 65–66
1. a) January b) March c) December d) June e) July f) May g) February h) April i) August j) October k) November l) September

Answers

Spelling Week 22 – Word Study, p. 67
Point to a random picture and ask for volunteers to name the season. Ask the class if they agree or disagree. Ask another volunteer to give the date they think that season starts. Ask the class if they agree or disagree. If there are any disagreements, ask for other suggestions.

Spelling Week 23 – Consonant Digraphs ch, sh, th, and wh, pp. 68–69
1. a) warmth b) who c) cheese d) think e) these f) teacher g) where h) finish i) shade j) children

Spelling Week 23 – Word Study, p. 70
1. a) when b) thunder c) shingles d) pinch e) wish f) chicken g) fifth h) cheap i) shimmer j) whisper k) thing l) splash
2. a) chip, ship, whip b) chick, thick c) with, wish d) chat, that, what e) then, when f) chin, shin, thin g) cheat, wheat h) chose, those, whose

Spelling Week 24 – Consonant Blends scr, spl, spr, and str, pp. 71–72
1. a) spray b) strange c) spring d) splash e) split f) scratch g) scrape h) strip i) stream j) strong

Spelling Week 24 – Word Study, p. 73
You may wish to ask a few children to share their stories with the class. Alternatively, you may wish to create a bulletin board display of children's stories.

Spelling Week 25 – Easily Misspelled Words, pp. 74–75
1. a) school b) people c) Another d) always e) until f) thought g) learn h) again i) many j) friend

Spelling Week 25 – Word Study, p. 76
You may wish to create a bulletin board display of children's pages, or have children share their pages with a partner.

Spelling Week 26 – R-controlled Vowels with or, er, ir, ur, and ear, pp. 77–78
1. a) world b) fear c) girl d) wear e) bird f) turn g) were h) burn i) fork j) here

Spelling Week 26 – Word Study, p. 79
1. er, ir, ur
2. a) Sample answers: ear, fear, wear, tear, sear, shear, pear, bear; b) 2 sounds
3. a) Learning new spelling words is fun! b) Give a smile and you'll get one back. c) You may wish to have students create their own secret messages and share them with a partner or in a group of four. Alternatively, you can ask volunteers for their secret message code, write it on the board, and decode the message as a class.

Spelling Week 27 – R-controlled Vowels with ar, are, or, and ore, pp. 80–81
1. a) sport b) normal c) fare d) shore, e) Aren't f) harm g) bored h) fork i) park j) more

Answers

Spelling Week 27 – Word Study, p. 82
1. a) apart b) bored c) floor d) hare e) pork f) spark
2. Sample answers: a) I take care of my pet rabbit every day. b) When John fell, he tore his jeans. c) I saw a shark at the aquarium. d) I love the smell of the air in the morning. e) Our neighbor has a very large dog named Max. f) My mother says it's not polite to stare. g) I always wash my hands before I eat. h) Getting ready for school only takes me a short time. i) My brother wants to be an astronaut and go to space when he grows up.

Spelling Week 28 – Words with an *f* Sound Spelled *ph, gh,* and *f*, pp. 83–84
1. a) favorite b) cough c) graph d) forget e) rough f) father g) phone h) Friday i) photo j) laugh

Spelling Week 28 – Word Study, p. 85
1. Sample answers: a) Something you like best b) To not remember something c) Something that is bumpy or scratchy
2. a) giggle b) bumpy c) picture d) dad
3. a) smooth b) remember c) cry d) disliked
4. Sample answers: a) tough, enough, buff, fluff, gruff b) graph, half, calf, staff

Week 29 – Words with Silent Letters, pp. 86–87
1. a) knife b) ghost c) climb d) sign e) write f) calm g) honest h) scent i) chalk j) guest

Spelling Week 29 – Word Study, p. 88
1. a) k and g b) h c) b d) l e) b f) e g) l h) b i) k and c j) h and u k) e l) b m) h and e n) c o) c and e p) g and e
2. comb, thumb, doubt, crumb
3. phone, airplane, rhyme, muscle, gnome
4. a) e, sale b) w, wrong c) k, knot d) b, lamb e) g, gnome f) l, walk g) g, light h) e, crane

Spelling Week 30 – Homophones, pp. 89–90
1. a) witch b) here c) knight d) write e) hear f) wear g) Which h) where i) right j) night

Spelling Week 30 – Word Study, p. 91
1. a) hair, hare b) hear, here c) stare, stair d) their, there e) pail, pale f) real, reel g) read, reed
2. a) hare b) stare c) pale d) sail e) reel f) reed g) heal

Amazing Work!
Spelling Superstar!

Great Effort!
Spelling Superstar!